Resisting Tyrants

Romans 13 and the Christian Duty to Oppose Wicked Rulers

GORDAN RUNYAN

ISBN-13: 978-1480220089

To the service of King Jesus, great King David's greater son.

INTRODUCTION

"Resistance to tyrants is obedience to God"
Thomas Jefferson

God bless America, land that I love. As of this day, July 26, 2012, these things are true in the "Land of the Free."

Kids have had their lemonade stands shut down for lack of a proper business license.

Farmers have been arrested for selling raw milk to their neighbors.

The President maintains a personally-written "kill list," a roll of names he has approved for summary assassination. The government admits that at least one American citizen has been put to death on the authorization of this list, without anything like a trial, due process of law, or even a warrant.

The new NDAA law, passed with strong, bipartisan support, gives the President the authority to have American citizens arrested and spirited away to prison, and detained indefinitely, without a trial or judicial oversight, on the suspicion of potential terrorism. Not *actual* terrorism. *Suspicion.*

For the sake of "protecting the public," agents of the TSA take naked-scan images of airline passengers and perform invasive grope-down searches randomly, searching the panties on little girls with their hands for explosives.

The Patriot Act allows federal agents to write their own search warrants, and authorize their own wiretapping operations against American citizens, completely bypassing 4th Amendment guarantees to judicial review, and the requirement for probable cause.

A section of the Marine Corps is being trained in domestic law enforcement. Think about that for a moment.

The FBI has admitted to hatching terror plots against the United States; then recruiting, funding, equipping, and training the would-be terrorists in these plots; and then stepping in at the last moment to arrest their co-conspirators, for the sake of being able to claim they are keeping America safe.

A judge in New Mexico has ordered a professional photography company to provide their private services to a same-sex couple getting married, though the company had tried to assert its free association rights and refuse their services for religious reasons.

A swarm of unelected bureaucrats blankets the land, sent out like a plague of locusts by the great god, EPA, to enforce laws and levy fines on property owners, rules which are practically made up on the spot, capricious laws which haven't come from Congress but still have the power to strip a citizen of livelihood and property.

The feds have begun building the Utah Data Center, which, by their own admission, is a gigantic project designed to capture and screen every single piece of electronic communication generated in the US.

The feds also admit to a plan to put up to 3,000 spy drones in the skies over America by 2020, not to foil any act in particular, but simply to keep watch on what the people are doing down there.

In its ruling on Obamacare this summer, the Supreme Court has agreed that the Federal government has an unlimited power to tax its citizens, even if those "taxes" amount to penalties applied to people who don't want to purchase products the government tells them to purchase.

And, finally, to this day unborn babies are murdered in America at a rate of about a million and a half each year, and this is done with the official sanction of the Federal government.

We'll stop here for now, but I wonder if your blood is boiling yet, Christian patriot?

There are two additional thoughts about this list that are especially aggravating. For one: This list is pitifully incomplete.

Space and time prevent us from documenting the government's daily transgressions against the Constitution and against the liberties which that ignored document preserves to American citizens. That would be a huge and ever-expanding book all by itself.

We've only hit some highlights. In fact, I've only included things that are out in the open. We all might have trouble sleeping at night if we knew the things they'd rather keep secret.

But secondly, and more disturbing: Aside from the plague of unjust government that now confronts this land, there is another. That is, our oppressed land is dotted with Gospel ministers and preachers who take pains to assure us that it is our Christian duty to render compliant servitude to the powers that be, which are responsible for the despotic things listed above.

A monumental task it is, indeed, to decide which of these two scourges in America is worse. Is it the secular governmental tyranny which extends its tentacles into every area of our lives? Or is it the Christian-ish cadre that tells us that God wants us to be a doormat for that tyranny?

The abomination from the sea or the abomination from the land? The Beast or the False Prophet, which is worse?

The one makes no bones about being your enemy as it seeks to crush all things under its feet. The other pretends to be your friend, your brother in Christ, as it instructs you that everything *you* love, as well, ought to be crushed in this manner, for this is God's good and gracious plan for you.

The patriots who won American independence from England would never have done so, if their preachers had been like most of ours. Instead of changing the world and creating the greatest nation on God's green earth, they would have been battered into slavish submission by preachers shouting at them, "Romans 13! Romans 13!"

American Evangelicals are fond of quoting the *Declaration of Independence* when it insists, "that all men are created equal, that they are endowed by their Creator with certain unalienable rights." Curiously, not as much fondness is found for quoting what comes later in the *very same sentence*: "That whenever any Form of Government becomes destructive of these ends, it is the Right of the People to alter or to abolish it."

The reason for this lack of fondness is, in order to get to the point of altering or abolishing a government, we'd first have to decide that a particular government had lost God's approval. And clearly we can't do *that*, as we're reminded again by the apologists for tyranny. Romans 13, after all!

But honestly, when we come right to the point, it doesn't matter who or what kind of preacher preaches it. The Christian believes that he must obey the Word of God, period.

If it is, in fact, true that Romans 13:1-7 teaches the people of God to offer unqualified obedience to tyrants, then that is what we must do. If the Word tells us to submit to evil, we'll be found rebels for opposing it.

However, the reverse holds as well. If Romans 13 actually teaches, contrary to most of our modern pulpits, that Jefferson got it right when he said, "Resistance to tyrants is obedience to God," well, then, *submitting to* and *serving* those same tyrants would be an act of treason against the King of kings.

[Please note: I've got no illusions about Thomas Jefferson's faith. Though Jefferson seems to have held to a form of theism, which included a profound respect for (portions of) the Bible, much of what he wrote argues against his having been a genuinely converted Christian.

But the folk proverb holds true in this case: even a blind squirrel can find a nut once in a while. This is especially so, if that unseeing animal happens to live in an area in which the overwhelming Christian culture has done a good job of scattering squirrel-food everywhere.]

In the remainder of this work, our discussion will divide in three parts, although you may note some necessary overlap. First, we will take a careful look at the Bible text in question, Romans 13:1-7. What does it really teach concerning submission to the government? Next, we will discuss issues related to the Christian duty to resist tyranny, including the answers to anticipated objections. Third, we'll try to see what all this means for us in the here and now.

The exposition that follows owes a great deal to the spade-work done in the 19th Century by James M. Willson, in his book *The Establishment and Limits of Civil Government*. That work is commended to the reader with the strongest possible enthusiasm.

Here is the full text in question, Romans 13:1-7, in the ESV.

Let every person be subject to the governing authorities. For there is no authority except from God, and those that exist have been instituted by God.

[2] Therefore whoever resists the authorities resists what God has appointed, and those who resist will incur judgment.

[3] For rulers are not a terror to good conduct, but to bad. Would you have no fear of the one who is in authority? Then do what is good, and you will receive his approval

, [4] for he is God's servant for your good. But if you do wrong, be afraid, for he does not bear the sword in vain. For he is the servant of God, an avenger who carries out God's wrath on the wrongdoer.

[5] Therefore one must be in subjection, not only to avoid God's wrath but also for the sake of conscience.

[6] For because of this you also pay taxes, for the authorities are ministers of God, attending to this very thing.

[7] Pay to all what is owed to them: taxes to whom taxes are owed, revenue to whom revenue is owed, respect to whom respect is owed, honor to whom honor is owed.

From the outset, every reasonable person would have to admit that, hypothetically, if the first two verses above were the only words we had from God on the matter of civil government, then the Christian-ish cadre would be correct. It would seem to mandate an unqualified obedience to all governing authorities.

But back in the real world, this passage has more to say than that, and so does the rest of God's inspired Book. We won't be excused for reading those first two verses as if they were isolated from the rest.

CONTEXT IS KEY

It's crucial in our study of the Bible to ask ourselves, "Now, why is this particular text in this particular place?"

It's good to understand what a text *says*, but even more so to understand *why* it says that, right *where* it says that. The context of Romans 13:1-7 is critical to understanding what it means.

Romans is the New Testament's great explanation of the Gospel of Jesus Christ. In the first eight chapters, Paul meticulously shows just how it is that sinners can be made right with God. He takes pains to prove that we are justified by faith in Jesus Christ, apart from works. He spends whole chapters (6-8) stressing that the Good News of salvation in Christ has set us free from slavish servitude to a Law that condemns sinners and demands their punishment.

"For the law of the Spirit of life has set you free in Christ Jesus from the law of sin and death." (Romans 8:2)

This had to have come as a bit of a shock to Paul's Jewish readers. Imagine.

They've spent their whole lives believing that it is their ability to keep God's Law, living their lives well in His sight, which forms the core of their religion, their racial identity, their culture, and the whole nation.

Along comes their long-expected Messiah, and turns all of that upside down, by insisting that a radically changed heart, a spiritual rebirth, and not law-keeping, is the key to entering the Kingdom of God. Certainly, this idea is going to bring thorough-going upheaval to the whole Jewish world!

And, yes, it certainly did. Paul spends the next three chapters in Romans 9-11 discussing the ramifications of this radical Gospel on the Jewish nation, Israel. What can it mean for them? What will become of them, now that the Christ has upset the apple-cart so?

Then, in chapter 12, Paul begins to list the everyday ramifications for the Christian believer. What should it mean to us, that we have been set free from condemnation? How should we then live?

Chapter 13, and our verses in question, come along right here, in this train of thought. How should the liberated believer live, specifically in relation to human governments?

It is plain to see why it would be prudent to answer this question. Throughout Israel's history, the Law of God was the government, for all intents and purposes. Sure, they had their kings, and judges, and ruling elders, but even all of *those* folks were under the authority of the Law. They were only subordinate rulers in Israel.

Truthfully, for the Jewish nation, to follow God's Law was to live under God Himself as their ultimate Sovereign. The Law of God was nothing other than the active *kingship* of God in Israel.

Now, fast-forward, along comes the promised Son of King David, to inherit the Kingdom and He institutes a New Covenant which sets all of His people free from the Law of God (at least, in its condemning, prosecuting function, though not from its morality.)

It's easy to imagine a Jewish person, freshly converted to faith in Christ, thinking like this:

"I used to be under the law. Now, Christ has set me free. Not under law but under grace. If I am no longer bound under the jurisdiction of the Law of God in this manner, then surely no merely *human* laws or governments can have any authority over me! If I'm free from servile life under God's own Law, how much less could any government of *man* command my service?"

And this is the sort of thinking (understandable, though wrong) which Paul sets about correcting as Romans 13 opens.

We note that, after chapter 13:1-7, we are given over two full chapters explaining that, although we have been set free from the Law's condemnation, that doesn't mean that we can live without restraint. Our liberty is not license. We still have good and righteous obligations, toward God and each other. It is clear: our new-found freedom in Christ comes with responsibilities, voluntary self-restraint, and a sense of repaying a debt of love (13:8.)

In the flow of this argument, how out-of-place it would be to have the Apostle suddenly break out with, "Oh, by the way, unrelated to anything we've been talking about, make sure you offer cheerful obedience to every despot, dictator, and tin-pot who crosses your path!"

That is not what he is saying in 13:1-7 at all. In fact, we mean to show that no tyrant is the subject of this passage. (They think they are, of course. They are like the man who is the subject of the old song, "You're So Vain," and they think this song is about them.) But, they are not mentioned, and are definitely not described. It's *not* about them.

What Paul teaches here is that the one who has been set free from terrified slavery to the Law of God cannot then take that freedom and set himself above the God-ordained institution of civil government. Government has a holy purpose, a fearful authority, and a mandate for its righteous mission that God has given.

ROMANS 13:1 – *"Let every person be subject to the governing authorities..."*

There are three terms in this phrase we need to consider closely. They are "governing," "authorities," and "subject."

Every person is to submit to the "governing" authorities. The word translated "governing" there by the ESV is the Greek word *huperecho*.

The word means to excel, to be superior, or better than; to surpass. The King James at this place has "higher powers," which makes room for the idea of being better than something else. The reason this is of some interest is that *huperecho* appears four other times in the New Testament.

One is in 1 Peter 2:13, in that letter's passage about civil government. The majority of uses occur, however, in Philippians, where Paul uses it three times, at 2:3; 3:8; and 4:7. These are quoted below. For ease of understanding, I've put the English words in ALL CAPS which are the renderings of *huperecho*.

Philippians 2:3 – "Do nothing from selfish ambition or conceit, but in humility count others MORE SIGNIFICANT than yourselves."

Philippians 3:8 – "Indeed, I count everything as loss because of the SURPASSING worth of knowing Christ Jesus my Lord. For his sake I have suffered the loss of all things and count them as rubbish, in order that I may gain Christ."

Philippians 4:7 – "And the peace of God, which SURPASSES all understanding, will guard your hearts and your minds in Christ Jesus."

As you can see, the Greek word means that which is morally better or excellent or weighty.

In these places, modern English translations usually have some combination of "important," "significant," and "surpassing" to translate *huperecho*. The KJV has "better," "excellency," and "passeth" (as in going beyond or surpassing) in the Philippians texts.

All this is simply meant to show that *huperecho* may legitimately refer to moral excellence, and does in fact, in most of its New Testament appearances. The modern use of "surpassing" in the Philippians passages is a moral surpassing. It is being better, rising above, doing well.

We want to be clear about this, and not say too much. The fact that the Greek word can refer to moral excellence is not the same thing as saying that's what it *must* mean everywhere it's used. It simply means it is a possible understanding. So that, when Romans 13:1 enjoins subjection to the *huperecho* powers, it's not out of the question that this could be referring to surpassing *morality*.

On this idea, Willson writes, "Hence, some expositors have been disposed to lay no little stress upon this epithet, as distinctly defining the character of the powers here intended, and as limiting to such the subjection here enjoined, the 'excelling powers;' that is, powers possessing a due measure of the qualifications requisite to the rightful exercise of the power of civil rule." [p.11, *The Establishment ana Limits oj Civil Government.*]

Some have suggested that to put "governing" instead of "higher" or "excelling" for *huperecho* in this place is really more of an interpretation than a word-for-word translation. They would contend that consistency demands that we translate the word the same way in this place as we have in the Philippians passages.

On the other hand, dictionaries and lexicons given all due respect, it is generally an accepted axiom that how a word is used is the chief determiner of what it means. Modern translators who have put "governing" for *huperecho* at Romans 13:1, instead of something like "morally excelling," would contend that government is the issue at hand in the passage, and therefore justifies the translation.

We probably won't settle this right here. Nevertheless, Willson is judicious in refusing to make a large issue of it. His, and our, exposition of the passage is too strong overall to need to quibble about how one word is translated. Let it stand as "governing" authorities. This is fine. The character of the authorities in view will be described in detail later, in undeniable language.

Moving on, when the passage speaks of powers or authorities, it speaks in a precise way. Meaning, the language at this point denotes a power that is given the right to enforce the law, but not to implement or execute its own will. And that is of some importance, that little distinction. If it's not given the right to do its own will, then whose will must it do? If its own word is not the law it should enforce, then whose law is?

To ask these questions is to answer them. The "powers" are meant to enforce God's will, God's laws, and not their own. We live in an age in which that is a violently "incorrect" answer (as in "politically incorrect,") and this is so even within the churches. As sad as that fact is, we can't modify the truth because of it.

As a last point of interest on the words that are used by the Holy Spirit in this verse, we note that the command to "be subject" or to "submit," is not what some might think. Some might imagine a puny kid getting pressed by the local bully for his lunch money. He initially says no. But getting slammed into the locker seems to change his mind, and he then passively reaches into his pocket and retrieves the cash. He hands it over, though with a dejected face.

This is not the sort of submission that is being recommended to the Christian here, the submission of one who has no real option but to go along for survival's sake. The word used here tells us that passive, grudging, non-resistance is not in view. We are not talking about one who must go along to get along. Rather, the term means, "voluntarily, freely, and cheerfully rendering allegiance and homage, and yielding a uniform and conscientious obedience to...wholesome laws." [ibid, p.12]

The bottom line of this first part of verse one is that God has instituted civil government in the world as His agency, to do His will. Further, since they are God's ministers, it is good and right for God's people to cheerfully obey them.

But please note, we haven't started talking about wicked governments yet; or, any particular, *actual* government at all. We're simply talking about the God-ordained *purpose* of human government.

ROMANS 13:1 *"... For there is no authority except from God, and those that exist have been instituted by God."*

This is a statement of the abstract idea of Providence. We stress "abstract" because we're still talking about the *theory* or the theology behind government. We haven't looked at any particular rulers yet.

The theology of government, in this case, is that God is King. He is the ultimate sovereign. He governs all things. All authority which we experience in this life is subordinate to God's final, ultimate authority. Another way to say it: all human authority is *derivative*. God institutes lesser authorities to do His will, to obey His own authority.

In addition, it is Biblically correct to acknowledge that all things that exist, do so by God's ordination, by His creation and will. Civil government is certainly a subset of all things which God has ordained. Civil rulers have power. All power comes from God.

Though the Scripture does not mention wicked government at this point, it's inevitable that we'll have to consider them when we think on these things. When we hear that God has willed the existence of all that exists, we ask out of reflex, "Even the bad things?"

And so it is here. Speaking on God's purposes and plans for human governments, we're reminded that all power, including civil authority, comes from God, and could not exist without Him. Yes, even the evil powers.

Wicked, idolatrous Pharaoh didn't raise himself to the throne. God takes credit for that (Romans 9:17.) The Lord raised up the king of Babylon; cast him down temporarily; and then restored him to his former position (Daniel 4.) He puts down one and exalts another. Jesus even said to the villainous politician, Pontius Pilate, when the latter asserted his authority over the former, "You would have no authority over me at all unless it had been given you from above. Therefore he who delivered me over to you has the greater sin." (John 19:11)

We mention this idea of God's providential rule over all things simply to make it clear: there is a sense in which all government that exists does so by the sovereign rule of God, as seen in His providence. Nothing that exists can exist *apart* from that rule, so we must acknowledge this point: even government that rebels against God does so according to His providence.

However, we must also take pains to press this corollary point: simply because a thing exists in the created world, as an expression of God's providential rule, that doesn't make it good. The fact that God has chosen to allow evil in this world for a time does not make that evil less evil.

Since evil things that exist by the permission of providence remain evil; and since God has spoken uniformly in the Bible to the effect that He expects His own people to hate all evil and to oppose that evil with good; then we must insist that we cannot take the mere existence of a thing as some sort of sign of God's approval of the thing.

God providentially allows evil in this world, but as Willson points out, "Providence is not a rule of action." [ibid, p. 21] That is, we must not make the mistake of observing what "is," and concluding that it "ought to be," simply because it "is."

"Is" does not equal "ought." Mere existence doesn't make a thing right. In fact, it is quite often wrong, and so the right thing to do (if we call ourselves the servants of a God who is Good) is to oppose that wrong.

Obvious examples of this can easily be multiplied, and it's a little embarrassing to have to list some, so obvious are they. And yet, we really must, because the state of modern Christianity is such that it needs, once again, to be instructed in first principles.

The devil exists, and wields great power, all under the will and authority of God. And yet, the people of God are commanded to resist him throughout the Scripture.

Ignorance of the true and living God abounds on the earth. This is a cataclysmic evil. And the *people* of God are commanded to oppose that evil through the preaching of the Scriptures.

Jesus empowered his first disciples to heal the sick and raise the dead, not to look upon disease and death as tokens of God's providential will, to remain unopposed.

Again, poverty is seen as a despicable evil from one cover of the Bible to the other: but the providential fact of its existence does not excuse the Christian from a duty to oppose it. He is everywhere commanded to fight against it through his own charitable giving and through instructing people how to make a living for themselves.

Here is the concept, stated simply: All things exist by the providential will of God. But their providential existence is not the same as having God's approval. Without understanding this vital distinction, Hosea 8:4 is unintelligible. There, the voice of God says, "They made kings, but not through me. They set up princes, but I knew it not."

Possessing authority that comes from God is not the same thing as possessing God's *sanction*, and approval to rule.

This is key. If we assert that God approves of all governing authority, regardless of how it came to be or what it does once it gets there, what we are really saying is that we think Might Makes Right. The mere fact that you have authority would have to mean God wants you to rule completely unopposed. This is not materially different from the old-world idea of the Divine Right of Kings. All lovers of liberty, and *especially* those who know their Bibles, should be repulsed by this idea.

As Willson decries concerning this ridiculous idea:

"No doctrine could be more agreeable than this to tyrants, and to all that panders to unholy power; for, if this be Paul's meaning, there is no despot, no usurper, no bloody conqueror, but could plead the divine sanction and, more than this, the devil himself could lay the teachings of Paul under contribution to enforce his pre-eminently unholy authority.

An interpretation which leads to such monstrous conclusions—that would bind the nations to the footstool of power with iron chains, and utterly crush every free aspiration—that would invest with the sanctions of the divine name the most flagrant usurpation and the most unrelenting despotism—stands self-condemned." [ibid, p.21]

It will be important for us to keep this concept in mind as we move on to look at the next verse in our passage. For now, let us conclude our discussion of Romans 13:1 with these bottom-line ideas clear in our minds:

1) The concept of civil government is God's idea, just as surely as are the concepts of church and family government. The Christian is required to yield whole-hearted and cheerful obedience to civil government, as it fulfills God's ordained intention for that government.

2) It is illegitimate for a Christian to use his freedom or liberty in Christ's gospel as a cloak for disobeying God's ordinance.

3) Though civil government, with regard to its *reason for being*, exists by God's design, that does not imply that all actual civil government is therefore to be considered Good. A government's mere *existence* does not automatically exempt it from godly *resistance*, as with many other things which Christians may be called to oppose, even though they exist for a time as expressions of the providential will of God.

Romans 13:2 *"Therefore whoever resis* *authorities resists what God has appointed, and* *those who resist will incur judgment."*

We happily admit in this place what has already been conceded above. That is, if these first two verses in our text were all we had in the Scripture concerning the relationship between God's people and civil government, we might well be forgiven for taking them as a straightforward statement that any and all resistance to any and all authority is condemned by God.

However, since that's not all we have in the Bible on the topic, that sort of leniency toward ignorance ought not be allowed.

Repeating ourselves here, but for the sake of stressing a vital point: these verses are speaking about government as a concept. Government as an idea. They are speaking of God's intended function of it. Nothing in the text would indicate that Paul has a particular government in view. Especially no particular, tyrannical one.

In this conceptual fashion, it is surely right to affirm that resisting what God has appointed will earn God's judgment. The Christian is not allowed to be an anarchist.

He must, if he's to be faithful to the Word of God, affirm a righteous purpose for governing authorities. To oppose that idea is to court God's just judgment.

hand, if we take this second verse
it that it is wrong to oppose any and
nmediately find ourselves set in
t of the Bible. Dear Christian, if
f the Scripture in any one place is
multiplied examples in other
places, you are simply wrong.

The Bible interprets itself. It is all in harmony.
You are convicted of error in the matter until you
modify your interpretation to do justice to all the data,
not merely what you think you have found at one point.

The Bible does not condemn all resistance to
wicked government in this place, only to repeatedly
show its heroes doing exactly that in many other places.
An incomplete list of examples follows (but that ought
to be enough.)

Moses and the people of Israel opposed, and
eventually destroyed, the lawful government of Pharaoh.
They had not been kidnapped, or brought there against
their will, but voluntarily. The government of Egypt
turned tyrannical against them over the course of several
centuries, and then God sent one (Moses) to oppose
that government, even to the point of its complete
destruction.

As a prelude to that story though, Scripture takes
special care to commend the faith of the Hebrew
midwives, who defied Pharaoh's command that the
Israelite children be exposed to death (Exodus 1:15-21.)
Disobedience to this same command by the parents of
Moses is immortalized as an act of great faith in
Hebrews 11:23.

Rahab, the Gentile harlot, is inducted into the "Hall of Fame of Faith" in Hebrews 11 for acting in a manner that her king would have, no doubt, considered treasonous. He wasn't asking anyone to commit a sin, but merely to keep him informed about the presence of spies in his own dominion. That's a reasonable request by any king. But she resisted him, and is blessed for it, not merely as mentioned above, but also in the epistle of James, at 2:25.

Let's not pass by that particular example too quickly. Twice in the New Testament (as every word is confirmed on the word of two or more witnesses) Rahab is listed as a heroic example of faith. Her obedience to God led her to oppose and resist the tyrant of Jericho, and this act of obedience/resistance finally led to his own destruction at Israel's hands.

We can be thankful that there are no such things as time machines. What a tragedy it would be if one of our modern, American Evangelicals travelled back to Jericho and had an opportunity to scold Rahab. "No, No! You must obey God's ordained authorities in all things lawful, or else earn His judgment!"

The book of Judges, likewise, furnishes all sorts of headaches for those Christian apologists for tyranny. Here is the repeated pattern in Judges.

God's people forget His laws and fall into rebellion.

God brings a foreign tyrant to put them in subjection. (Thus giving the rebellious people the "government they deserve.")

These tyrants become the established, recognized rulers over the land.

God's people eventually cry out in their oppression and hardship.

God then raises up a deliverer, called a "judge."

The judge leads the people to resist the tyrant in power. And not only so, but this repeatedly means casting off and killing the tyrant through the use of military force.

The people then enjoy a period of peace under the ruling influence of this judge.

We stress that several of these judges join Rahab in the roll of heroes mentioned in Hebrews 11. The Bible has left no doubt about the opinion of God with regard to their actions, to the consternation of those without backbones everywhere: the Holy Spirit calls them "men of whom the world was not worthy." They do not incur His judgment, but His public blessing.

In 1 Kings 21, Ahab the king (God's ordained, governing authority, let's be reminded) makes his relationship to Elijah the prophet perfectly clear. He knows that Elijah is his "enemy" (v.20) and the prophet takes no pains to try and correct that assessment, but rather gives reason for affirming it. Ask Ahab if he thinks Elijah is yielding a Romans 13 sort of cheerful, voluntary obedience to God's governing authority! He will laugh in your face, and probably go on to detail why he refers to the prophet as "the troubler of Israel!"

Every child who's spent any time in Sunday School has heard, and re-heard, the stories of Daniel and his friends defying the king of Babylon. As well, the story of the apostle Peter defying the Sanhedrin (a lawfully constituted, civil authority in first century Jerusalem) by asserting that he had to obey God and not men (Acts 5:29.)

But, the modern Evangelical interpretation of Romans 13:1-2 would have us believe the two are the same: the laws of the human government and the will of God. To defy the former is to earn the judgment of the latter, if the spineless ones are correct here.

We've only scratched the surface. We won't belabor the point. But the point should nonetheless be clear:

The rest of the Bible will not allow us to assert that it is always wrong to defy human governments. In fact, it is right to go further: sometimes biblical faith *demands* that we resist the tyrants. We have seen that demonstrated repeatedly in the few examples above.

All that Romans 13:2 is saying, therefore, is that the concept and existence of civil government is a righteous thing that comes from God. We cannot be anarchists. Governing authorities are a good idea, and to be found in opposition to that concept is to call for judgment from God.

ROMANS 13:3-4 *"For rulers are not a terror to good conduct, but to bad. Would you have no fear of the one who is in authority? Then do what is good, and you will receive his approval, for he is God's servant for your good. But if you do wrong, be afraid, for he does not bear the sword in vain. For he is the servant of God, an avenger who carries out God's wrath on the wrongdoer."*

In verse One above we saw that God has established civil authorities to enforce not their own will, but His. Since they are to enforce His will, all of His people should render their voluntary, willing, heartfelt obedience.

In verse Two, the apostle reminds us that all authority comes from God and therefore civil authority deserves to be respected as coming ultimately from Him. To do otherwise is not wise.

Now, in verses Three and Four, the apostle begins to list exactly what these former truths ought to look like when they happen in real life. He describes in greater detail what the legitimate, governing authority ought to resemble.

The first, and probably most important thing to note right off the bat is that the ruler in question is described as the "servant" of God twice. Many have pointed out that the word translated *servant* is the same word that is translated *deacon*, when the Bible speaks of servants within the church. Literally, Paul is calling the ruler God's deacon.

If the ruler is God's servant, His deacon, then whose will ought he be about the business of enforcing? Whose definitions of right and wrong should he use as he decides who needs to be punished?

The current, cultural proverb applies here: *This ain't rocket science!* Only the man with an agenda could come up with the wrong answer.

God's servant ought to serve **God.** Well, *duh*, say the kids.

Now think for a moment about a ruler who refuses to serve God. He is not faithful to Him, in word, thought or deed. He sneers at the Lord's laws; he considers himself too evolved for them, maybe. He uses his office to serve himself. Is this the sort of government that Paul is describing here?

Again, it's a question that is answered once it's asked, by everyone with a functioning brain in their heads. Tyrants and dictators cannot be found in this passage.

So, with the use of the word "deacon" and the epithet, "servant of God," it becomes quite clear the character of the ruler who is in view in this passage.

In addition, we see a great deal concerning the particular mission of civil government. This, sadly, is also a place that modern Evangelicalism needs to sit at the apostle's feet and learn a lesson or two.

We have been swayed as a culture by the slow infiltration of positivist theories of government. They've come to us in strains of Marxism, socialism both hard and soft, and outright communism.

So pervasive has this unholy influence been, it is tough to find a single, professed "conservative" who rejects the idea that government should be a do-gooder and a problem-solver. Government has become the closest thing to a Messiah for many in our day: and those who worship it pray to it constantly to come and make all things new for them.

However, God opposes this notion by setting out not only the authority of civil government, but also the definition of its God-given mission. We are not free as Christians to make our governments what we think they ought to be. Their reason for existing, as well as their existence itself, is from God.

That mission is pitifully simple, direct, and straightforward. Which is probably why so many meddlers are tempted to start messing with it.

The servant/ruler is made to "bear the sword" as "an avenger who carries out God's wrath on the wrongdoer."

Wrongdoing constitutes an attack upon the rights and the peace of the people. The ruler/deacon is given the "sword," an emblem of physical force and violence, in order to function as the conduit of the wrath of God upon those who trouble the people, trampling their God-given rights (whether through domestic crime or military invasion from outside.)

Nothing is stated here, or anywhere else in the Bible, for that matter, which would expand the rights of the State beyond this simple mandate. Punish wrongdoing, with the sword if necessary. Once in a while, maybe, catch somebody being righteous and recognize them for it in some small way. Protect the good guys from the bad guys. Just do that, and we'll all be happy.

Nothing is said about the civil State becoming the educator, or the banker, or the doctor, or the charitable outlet, or the babysitter, or the consumer advocate of the people. A ruler who takes one of these duties to himself has become a ruler who has abandoned his God-given mission. And he will answer for that.

Punish wrongdoing. Punish it according to the definitions of Good and Evil that we find everywhere in the Word of the God who has empowered you. Just do that!

A COUNTER ARGUMENT CONSIDERED

In our day there are those who would dispute our interpretation at this point. They would say, Look, Paul was living under the rule of the Roman Empire when he wrote these words. Specifically, he wrote to Roman Christians who had Caesar Nero as their king. And see how he chooses to describe them! He still sees them as God's servants, and still commends them for exacting God's vengeance on wrongdoers. So, the argument goes, if Paul could still call the Roman government God's servant, then how much more should we acknowledge that our own civil rulers (admittedly less evil than Nero) are to be completely obeyed?

But this is a classic example of "assuming what you need to prove." They merely *declare* that Nero and Rome are being described here. Once they have declared it so, they use the supposed truth of their declaration to drive home their argument. We are right, because we *say* we are; and therefore your interpretation must be wrong.

That may pass for Biblical argument in some quarters, but a few of us hard-headed types remain unimpressed.

Confident declarations aside, we'd like to see some *proof* that Paul had those villains in mind when he spoke of servants of God who praise the good and punish the wicked. A mere assertion will not suffice, precisely because we see the Bible elsewhere describing *this particular government* in very different terms.

Daniel, for instance, predicted this Roman Empire and described his vision of it in chapter 7 of his prophecy. He writes, "After this I saw in the night visions, and behold, a fourth beast, terrifying and dreadful and exceedingly strong. It had great iron teeth; it devoured and broke in pieces and stamped what was left with its feet. It was different from all the beasts that were before it, and it had ten horns." (Daniel 7:7)

In its context, this beast is one that is considered an enemy of God, not His deacon. In addition to the Daniel passage, many commentators on the Revelation see this same Roman Empire described in that book, as the dragon clothed with human, governmental power (heads, horns, and crowns) in ch. 12; or as the beast from the sea in ch. 13; or as the beast on which the harlot rides in ch. 17. These descriptions of first-century Rome, whether from Daniel 7 or from some such place in the Revelation, stand 180 degrees out from the description of "God's servant" in Romans 13:3-4.

If there was any doubt about this, history proves us vindicated by the manner in which things played out. Is there even a remote possibility that Paul would speak of the same government which murdered Christ by calling it God's *deacon*? Who would not laugh such an idea out of court?

Early Christian tradition has it that the Empire also put to death Peter and Paul, the two foremost ministers of the Gospel in the generation after Christ. We are supposed to believe that this government is described at all in Romans 13? There is a technical, theological term for that idea: Baloney!

Paul recommends that his readers simply do the right things and they'll have nothing to fear from the civil rulers. Could he have been thinking about Nero's Rome when he said that? Not a chance, for the same Paul, according to the earliest witnesses, was beheaded precisely for doing good; and furthermore, under the reign of Nero, we know that many thousands of Christians in Rome were executed for proclaiming faith in Christ! It is astounding that some would have us believe Paul was describing this government when he spoke of God's servant, who is **no threat to good works.**

In concluding this section, we summarize our findings. God has ordained the institution of civil government.

He has also given it its only legitimate marching orders, a narrow and simple mission: to do His will, by serving Him in the prosecution of His own rules of righteousness, against all wrongdoers.

In Romans 13:3-4 we therefore see the description of that government to which Christians are compelled to yield cheerful, voluntary, whole-hearted obedience. It is the one that is actually setting out to perform that mission!

There is nothing in this about serving tyrants, or offering them a passive non-resistance. To insert a wicked government into this Bible text not only overturns the text itself, but would end up committing spiritual treason, by giving aid and comfort to the enemies of God and His Christ. Surely no one having the Spirit of God within would receive an idea like that with anything other than revulsion.

ROMANS 13:5 *"Therefore one must be in subjection, not only to avoid God's wrath but also for the sake of conscience."*

This verse doesn't need the same sort of discussion as the previous ones. Once we understand the four verses above, and have it straight in our minds the sort of government they are describing, the idea in this verse flows naturally.

A government that is working (imperfectly, we would even grant) to do the right things by enforcing godly laws, has every right to the support and subjection of its Christian citizens. Those citizens ought to find their consciences troubling them if they fail in this regard.

It is very similar to the Christian's approach to his own church. Surely, our churches are imperfect. As the Westminster divines recognized, even the best congregations under heaven are mixtures of truth and error, and there are tares in every wheat field. If you find a perfect church, don't join it, because you'll mess it up with your own imperfection.

But an imperfect church can still be a true and genuine church. For proof, we only have to read Paul's letters and see that he addresses those as churches, and saints, who are manifestly messed-up in many areas. Some have *seriously* put their doctrinal carts before their horses; some have square wheels on the carts, and carts made of meatloaf, etc. Still, they are really churches, loved by Christ.

In the same way, we are not demanding perfection in a human government before we will yield to it. Stumbling along and even faltering in the path can be excused, as long as we're faltering on the *right* path! Missing the mark may be tolerated so long as we really are trying to hit the target.

Where is that line? Where shall we distinguish between rulers who are on the right path, though failing badly at times, and those who have forsaken the way altogether, and now deserve only righteous opposition? Are we ruled by good powers acting poorly (as with King David in the Bathsheba incident,) or evil powers waxing worse and worse? The line is maybe not as bright as we'd like it to be, but, frankly, that is no excuse for acting like no one can possibly see it, ever.

To lay all the cards on the table, I believe that the list of offenses that are being perpetrated on the American public at this hour (with which this little book began) is incontrovertible evidence of a government in full rebellion against God. It is not a good government making mistakes. It is tyrannical and wicked. *For me, the line is crossed.*

My fellow Christian patriots, especially those pastors and leaders in the churches, will need to make their own prayerful evaluations, begging for God's wisdom, as in James 1:5.

But there is simply no way to view the description of God's intention for government, and find that somehow exemplified in modern America. Only someone intentionally seeking to provide cover for the tyrants could do so.

ROMANS 13:6-7 *For because of this you also pay taxes, for the authorities are ministers of God, attending to this very thing. Pay to all what is owed to them: taxes to whom taxes are owed, revenue to whom revenue is owed, respect to whom respect is owed, honor to whom honor is owed.*

The government that does the will of God in its opposition to evil and praise of the good, has a right to financial support for that very enterprise. They are the ones "attending to this very thing."

Which thing? That whole **obeying God** thing. There is, therefore, a lawful and honorable sort of taxation, at least in theory.

Since, as I have confessed above, I think the American swarm of rulers is in clear rebellion, *I don't think they are in view here at all.*

When they tax, it is not honorable, or lawful. When they tax the people it is theft, just as surely as their own claim to power is usurpation.

Does that mean I think individual Christians should stop paying taxes in America? No; because, when the guy robbing you blind has a gun barrel stuck in your face, and a publicly demonstrated history of willingness to use it, the better part of valor is to give away your wallet and live to fight another day, and continue to protect your loved ones, until the circumstances of the fight may be more to your advantage.

Some may take another course, but it's pretty clear the jack-boots will come for you as soon as you don't pay what they think you owe. They'll bring more guns than you have, count on it. They put Al Capone away on tax violations charges. You ain't got the resources Capone had, or the agents secretly paid off that he had. They got *him*: and *you* are small potatoes. Pick which hill you want to die on. I say, pay the thief, and use your current freedom from prison to expose and oppose the tyrants in every God-honoring way on the outside. Teach, exhort, and educate your children and neighbors. Most of all, Christian patriot, pray and preach. This is the Biblical recipe for turning things upside down.

It is possible, according to the text, for a government to require a tax that is honorable, that obeys God, and that ought to be paid by God's people for the sake of conscience. We've talked above about one way for that government to go off the rails and start requiring unjust taxation: that is, the abandonment of their God-given station and mission.

Unjust government cannot collect a just tax, no matter how they label it. A spectator at a football game can't penalize a team by throwing his own yellow hanky onto the field, even if he throws it just like a *legitimate* referee would. Even if he really saw a foul on the field, he still can't do this, because he is not the ref. Likewise, unjust government is not God's deacon, and therefore has no legitimate right to the money earned by God's people, even if it seems to be going through the right motions.

Our verse also speaks of honor and tribute and respect, etc. It is right for the Christian citizen to offer these all up to the civil magistrate who is actually trying to do what God has sent him to do. In a monarchy, for instance, which was ruled by a king who feared God, and governed accordingly, if the established custom was to honor this king with titles like "Your royal highness," or with a reverent bow, not only would it be okay for the Christian citizen to render these things, but he is actually required (as we've said repeatedly above) to submit himself to all of this with a cheerful and willing spirit, not grudgingly or as if under protest.

SUMMARY OF THE EXPOSITION OF ROMANS 13:1-7

We have seen why this passage exists at all, and why Paul placed it where he did in the overall flow of the epistle. He was answering an objection that he anticipated, one that might be asked by a Christian convert from life-long Judaism.

Those ancient Jews had struggled in slavish fear under the shadow of the Law of God for millennia. They lived and died under its jurisdiction. As soon as they broke any portion of it, it condemned them as sinners, liable to God's awful punishment.

But there was astonishing freedom to be found through the Gospel of Jesus Christ. By trusting in Him, and forsaking their own pitiful attempts at righteousness (law-keeping) they became united with Him. His death became theirs. His resurrection brought them new life. (See Romans 6, especially.) And their relationship to the Law of God necessarily changed. The Law previously convicted them as law-breakers worthy of death, and in the substitutionary sacrifice of Jesus, that sentence was fully carried out.

In the new life they had been given by Christ, the Law no longer held the same condemning power over them. They were free!

Now, upon hearing these things, it is reasonable to guess that some among them may have been tempted to think, "If I'm free from the jurisdiction of the Law of God, surely no mere law of *man* can command my submission!"

Paul's answer to that line of thinking is not complex. The same God who has released you from the Law's condemnation has also ordained civil governments, for a good and honorable purpose. The civil ruler is to be His servant, His deacon, for the punishment of evil and the praise of those who do good.

To the degree the civil ruler uses his God-given authority to carry out this mission in service to God, you, Christian freed-man, are obligated to submit to him with a willing mind; not in grudging obligation, like a slump-shouldered teen doing a gallows-march to his room to clean it, as he's been asked.

As the ruler faithfully pursues this ministry of his, he will require financial resources, and so has been authorized to levy taxes, which you must pay. In all other good ways, as well, the servant of God who is so engaged in prosecuting His will, is worthy of your respect and honor.

Nothing in the entire passage has any reference to wicked rulers. It says not word one about rebellious magistrates; or those who oppose God; or those who become despotic and tyrannical in their abuse of power. None of these sorts of governments are addressed or described here at all. Rather, the whole point of the passage is simply to clarify that there is indeed a God-ordained purpose for civil government.

Now, if it is correct that wicked rulers are not addressed here, then does that mean the passage has nothing to say to us about how to deal with them? No, it doesn't mean that.

Many Bible teachers of the past, including John Calvin, for instance, have recognized a particular feature of God's commandments. And that is, when He gives us a commandment in the form of Thou Shalt Not, there is a parallel, corresponding, positive duty that, although unspoken, is nonetheless quite real.

It's easiest to explain this concept by illustration. For instance, when the Sixth Commandment tells us, "Thou shalt not kill," there is more to it than merely the prohibition on murder. Though unmentioned, the corresponding positive duty commands us as well.

That is, it's not just that we can't kill each other; it is also that we have a positive duty to protect and defend each other's lives, as we may see them threatened. If I am in a situation where I can take action to save your life, but I allow you to be killed, I'm guilty of breaking the Sixth Commandment even if I'm not the one who killed you.

When the Eighth Commandment tells us not to steal from each other, there is a positive duty that is also involved. Not only can't I pilfer your wallet, but if I find it on the ground where you dropped it, then I have a positive duty, according the Eighth Commandment, to protect your wallet for you and get it back to you.

The negatively stated commandment that tells me not to lie, is at the same time a *positive commandment* (though unspoken) to tell the truth. You see how that works.

It goes in the other direction as well. If you are given a *positive* duty in the Word of God, there are unspoken *restrictions* that we're also supposed to understand.

One example of this is found in Mark 10:2-9. Jesus is asked about divorce, and whether it's lawful. His answer cited the *positive injunction* from God concerning the first marriage, of Adam and Eve, in Genesis 2.

"Therefore a man shall leave his father and mother and hold fast to his wife, and the two shall become one flesh." (Mark 10:7-8)

Jesus then went on to use this positive statement about the origin of marriage to explain that it always carried with it a *corresponding restriction against divorce*: "What therefore God has joined together, let not man separate." (Mark 10:9)

Positive command: A man shall leave father and mother and hold fast to his wife.

Corresponding negative (though originally left unspoken): You should not be divorced.

This principle of unspoken correspondence applies throughout the Bible, in all of its commands. It works with promises and threatening as well. If God promises to bless a man, then that man begins to defy God, the man will not be blessed but rather cursed, probably with the corresponding opposite of the original blessing. (See Ezekiel 18, for a discussion of this kind of thing.)

With this concept in mind, let's consider again what God commands in Romans 13:1-7. **Submit cheerfully to rulers who are serving God in the execution of His will against evil-doers.**

That's the positive command. But what if we replace some words about those rulers, and instead have them as those "who are defying God in flagrant rebellion against His will?" Then what must we do to the phrase "submit cheerfully" in order to maintain correspondence? Surely no mind captured by the Word of God would suggest we ought to leave them that way!

I suggest that the corresponding, opposite term for *submit* has to be something like *resist*. That only makes sense.

But, frankly, I'd keep the adverb *cheerfully*. We should resist *cheerfully*, because it simply won't do for God's people to serve Him with sadness. Obedience to God, for the New Testament believer, is not a sour, dour, bitter thing. It is a joy.

Let us obey the Lord by resisting tyrants cheerfully!

This is soundly Biblical, and the Bible-trained heart will hear the refrain and want to shout:

Let the godly exult in glory;
let them sing for joy on their beds.
Let the high praises of God be in their throats
and two-edged swords in their hands,
to execute vengeance on the nations
and punishments on the peoples,
to bind their kings with chains
and their nobles with fetters of iron,
to execute on them the judgment written!
This is honor for all his godly ones.
Praise the LORD! (Psalms 149:5-9)

PART TWO: ADDRESSING OBJECTIONS

Objection: "But, didn't Jesus say we're supposed to 'render unto Caesar?'"

Yes, Jesus did say that. And your *point* is....? (That's my snarky way of saying there's nothing about this statement that modifies what we've said above about Romans 13.) Let's look at this.

Here is the full text being referred to, from Matthew's account of the incident:

Then the Pharisees went and plotted how to entangle him in his words.

And they sent their disciples to him, along with the Herodians, saying, "Teacher, we know that you are true and teach the way of God truthfully, and you do not care about anyone's opinion, for you are not swayed by appearances. Tell us, then, what you think. Is it lawful to pay taxes to Caesar, or not?"

But Jesus, aware of their malice, said, "Why put me to the test, you hypocrites? Show me the coin for the tax."

And they brought him a denarius. And Jesus said to them, "Whose likeness and inscription is this?"

They said, "Caesar's."

Then he said to them, "Therefore render to Caesar the things that are Caesar's, and to God the things that are God's."

When they heard it, they marveled. And they left him and went away. (Matt 22:15-22)

What we have here, as Matthew is careful to tell us, is an attempt to trick Jesus into getting Himself in trouble with His own words. We have a trick question responded to with an intentionally vague answer.

Let's take a moment to see how that is. First we see that the Pharisees devised a trick question, and sent two groups to Jesus to ask it. That is, they sent their own disciples, and the Herodians. It's of some importance to understand how these two groups were different.

The Pharisees were the religious conservatives of the day. They were zealous for returning to, and maintaining, the traditions that made Jews Jewish.

From a political standpoint, this group was anti-Roman. They were generally milder in their opposition to the Empire than the Zealots, however, who were itching for armed rebellion. Still, they were constantly irritated by the idea of the people of God, and the Promised Land, being ruled by pagan idolaters.

Then there were the Herodians. They get their name from Herod, which was the family name of the Edomites who had been set up by the Romans as kings over Judea and surrounding regions. They were Roman puppets. The group that is called the Herodians was thus a group of Jews in Israel who, for political reasons, were supporters of the puppet-king. Their whole livelihood was from the Romans, and they knew it. There was no more pro-Roman group among the Jews, therefore.

So we have the anti-Empire Pharisees teaming up for this incident with the staunchly pro-Empire Herodians, and their question is designed to trap Jesus into having to repudiate one group or the other. Here is the dilemma they thought to trap him in:

If Jesus answered that Caesar should not be paid taxes, well then, though the common crowd would like that response, the Herodians would be there to witness it, and then would be able to report back as eye-witnesses to the Nazarene's seditious teaching!

On the other hand, if Jesus advocated paying taxes to Caesar, he would surely lose a great deal of stature in the eyes of the common people, who tended to agree with the Pharisees about Roman rule. Jesus might even earn Himself a reputation as a sympathizer with the Empire.

So, answer one way, and Jesus becomes liable to charges of lawless rebellion against Caesar. Answer the other way, and He stands to lose support among the people. Either outcome is a big win for His enemies.

Jesus escapes this seemingly tight snare with amazing ease. He asks for a coin, and an identification of the image on it, and then famously says, render to Caesar what is his, and to God what is His.

This sent both of the conspiring groups away scratching their heads, no doubt. It's a famous answer; it's a brilliant answer, a verbal beat-down for the ages; and it is also quite *vague*.

So, when the Evangelicals come to us saying, "Render unto Caesar," we have a right to raise a polite finger and start asking some questions, for the sake of clarification. What exactly does that mean? Exactly *what belongs to Caesar*, so that we may render it? And in the American system of government, who or what corresponds to Caesar, if anything?

These are not diversionary questions, designed to help us delay obedient rendering. They *must* be answered, or no obedience is even possible.

Let's ask again and try to work through some answers. Give Caesar what is his. Okay. So what is *his?* Well, in the actual event, you could tell that the *coin* legitimately belonged to Caesar because it bore Caesar's image. But, as Douglas Wilson is fond of pointing out, as a created human being, Caesar himself is stamped with the image of God. And so, if image-bearing marks ownership here, then the coin must be rendered to Caesar, but Caesar *himself* must be rendered unto God!

This is a clever way of pointing to a Biblical truth that has tremendous bearing with regard to Christ's statement. That truth is this: All things belong to God. This isn't even up for negotiation. It is a bedrock axiom: The entire shootin' match is His.

To quote just one place where this total ownership is set down, Psalms 24:1 says, "The earth is the Lord's and the fullness thereof, the world and those who dwell therein."

Jesus didn't merely say, "Render unto Caesar." He also said, "Render unto God."

As someone has presciently said, "If we really rendered unto God everything that is His, there would be nothing left for Caesar."

Thus we see the real brilliance of Jesus' statement. The Herodians walked away having to admit that He had seemed to allow for paying the tax; but any perceptive students of the Word would've understood what He just said: It's all God's.

Jesus wasn't advocating a tax revolt here, either. He Himself at another time (Matthew 17:24-27) paid a tax that He had no obligation to pay, for the sake of avoiding undo offense. (Which I take to be a wise strategy at the present time, as I've suggested above.)

At the very least, though, His teaching at this point would seem to put some pretty severe limitations on what may be rendered to Caesar. And again we ask the Evangelical, *What belongs to Caesar?*

Surely the king doesn't get to touch his finger to any ol' thing he pleases and say, "Mine!" It would be the height, or maybe the depth, of foolishness to agree to "render unto Caesar" and then give *Caesar* the privilege of declaring what it his. If you imagine he might voluntarily, out of a good heart, limit his own reach and authority to the sort of small circle that reflects the Biblical teaching on what kings should and shouldn't do....well, then, out here in the high plains desert of eastern New Mexico, I've got a bridge to sell you.

You, Evangelical, the one who thinks "render unto Caesar" is some sort of blanket command to obey the government in all things, you tell me: What if Caesar places his finger on your children and says they belong to him?

What if he places it on your chosen career path and claims to know what job you, and your spouse, ought to be performing in his service?

Or that he needs your second car more than you do, or that he doesn't think you need to own a firearm, or that he wants to have you host two officers in his military service indefinitely in your home, at your expense?

Maybe it's your church that Caesar decides is his, to manage and control? He needs all your sons to fight in his wars. Come to think of it, he'll have all your daughters for the same purpose as well.

I know, I know. Some of the more faux-pious sort out there will go through that list and think, "I could survive all of that and go along with it if I knew that righteousness demanded it of me."

Well, duh.

That's just the point: Nowhere in God's book are kings allowed to act like that (although they do so, shaking their fists at God.) And so, since God doesn't *allow* it, righteousness does not demand it of you! What the righteousness of God, as defined in His Book, the Bible, demands from cover to cover from the people of God is that they stand firm in the evil day.

We are to take our stand against the world rulers of this present darkness, clothed in the armor of God. The devil prowls around like a roaring lion, and you and I are **not** told to acquiesce to his demands, but rather to **resist him**, firm in the faith. Stare down the enemies of our God with lion-like courage, fearing not the face of man, whether kings or princes.

In short, we ought to "play the man." And may God be pleased to rid us even in our day from sissified, Christianish, play-time religion.

My answer to my own question: What belongs to Caesar? Only what God *says* belongs to Caesar.

And where might we find those kinds of instructions? Well, honestly, there are several places we could look. Call me biased, but after writing twenty-some-odd pages explaining it, my mind is automatically drawn to Romans 13:1-7!

God has not only ordained that there should be such a thing as civil government, but He has also clearly defined the boundaries of its mission. The ruler is to execute God's wrath vs. evil-doers, which will tend to increase the peace and prosperity of those who do good. In the prosecution of this mission, the ruler may lay claim to the needed resources. Once he steps outside those boundaries, though, anything that he claims is his is only one more thing he is trying to steal.

Another crucial question to address in this regard is: In the current, American system of governance, who, or what, is Caesar?

To answer this, we need to remind ourselves that in his own context, Caesar was the top dog, the head honcho, *El Guapo*. The whole Roman Empire was centered on him, its emperor. No Caesar, no Empire. Rome certainly had its bureaucratic system, with scads of officials, and oodles of operatives. But Caesar sat at the top of the heap. There was no aspect of Roman government that was higher.

In America, it was part of the genius of the founders that they specifically avoided a system in which any one man sat at the pinnacle like that. However, that doesn't mean that the pinnacle is unoccupied, just because no *man* sits there.

The highest law of the land in America is the US Constitution. Hopefully, I've not sprung a surprise on anybody by saying so.

The President, along with each of the Supreme Court justices and every member of Congress, take oaths to uphold, to protect and defend the Constitution. The whole form of American government hangs on this principle, at least by design. In practice, we've, um, moved some of the furniture around a bit.

Again, not intending to surprise with this, the US Constitution is a type of thing known as a limited-powers document. What that boils down to is this: As written, the intention was that the Federal government would have no authority, and no power, that was not expressed explicitly. If it didn't say the government *could* do thing X, then it *may not do* thing X, even if a bunch of smart people tell us that thing X is the best darned thing to come around since at least the time of thing W.

With these basic points in mind, my suggestion is that, in America, "rendering to Caesar" would have to mean making sure that the government stays within the confines of the Constitution. When Congress makes laws arrogating to itself the authority to regulate the way a farmer farms his own land, it is in fact disobeying the American "Caesar" in order to do so, because the Constitution gives it no such authority. When the Federal government ignores or violates the Constitution, then somebody who knows a thing or two about the Bible ought to "have a cow about it" as the kids say, and demand that we render unto Caesar!

Objection: "But, wasn't Paul living under a worse tyranny than we've ever imagined when he urged submission to the government?"

This objection came up in the body of the exposition of Romans 13:1-7 above. We won't repeat the answer in detail here, except to note that this: If Paul had the current Empire in mind, his instructions to his readers turned out to be disastrous. He said, do good, and you will not need to fear the sword. In fact, you'll receive praise from the governor. In reality, the Christians followed his instructions, did what was right, and met with the sword, as many thousands of them were executed on Nero's orders, for no crime other than following Christ.

They got the opposite of what Paul predicted they would get. They did what was good and got the sword, which is not at all what Paul said would happen. So this objection causes a bigger problem than it is meant to solve: *now* you must deal with the fact that Paul wrote false prophecy. Do we need something more in order to reject this idea?

Objection: "But, instead of Resisting Tyrants, shouldn't we submit where we can, and only resist if we are ordered to sin?"

There are several reasons why this sort of neither-here-nor-there strategy is hopelessly unworkable.

First, that kind of submission being proposed is quite different than the kind that is commanded by God in Romans 13:1. The Scripture in that place (as we saw above in the exposition) commands a willing and even cheerful obedience. It is obedience not only in action, but in the mind and from the heart.

Second, cheerfully obeying a command is axiomatically an admission that the one making the command has the authority to do so. Since lying is a sin, last time I checked anyway, for me to act as if the tyrant is a genuine and lawful authority is to bear false witness about it.

Third, to wait to resist until I am ordered to sin is like waiting to be concerned about the cleanliness of my favorite restaurant until the moment I sit down to order food. It's like knowing there's a dead fly in my soup and continuing to eat around it. It's like putting up with a false teacher in your church, so long as he keeps talking about stuff you can agree with him on.

Fourth, if the devil himself handed you a postcard and asked you to drop it in the mail for him, would you do it? Why not? Dropping off mail at the Post Office is no sin, right? So why not? Well, because *he's the devil*, and Christians are called to resist him, not do what he asks as long as it isn't a sin. In the same way, a wicked ruler is an abomination. Proverbs 16:12 (NASB) says, "It is an abomination for kings to commit wicked acts, for a throne is established on righteousness." *Abomination.* Period. Whether he's executing believers, or playing a friendly game of Canasta, it doesn't matter. He's a wicked king, and therefore an enemy of God. We're called to resist evil, not let it take us as far as we feel comfortable with.

Fifth, there is something conveniently self-centered about this proposed strategy. "Wait to resist until *I personally* am ordered to sin." While you wait for the moment the government tells you to renounce Christ, your neighbors and fellow citizens are being trampled by the unrestrained, unjust use of power.

Today, as I write this, I read the report of a farmer who began serving a 30 day jail sentence for the crime of collecting rainwater that had fallen on his own land. And something close to 3,000 babies will be dismembered in the womb or burned to death in a salt solution today, with the government's sanction and the assistance of taxpayer money. As the Scripture says, "Like a roaring lion or a charging bear is a wicked ruler over a poor people." (Proverbs 28:15) But, hey, as long as *you personally* haven't yet been commanded to blaspheme God, I guess we can all breathe easy. As William Wilberforce said, "A private faith that does not act in the face of oppression is no faith at all."

Objection: "Christians should not get tangled up in politics, but should rather focus on preaching the Gospel."

I would be very happy to agree to this if it were even possible. But in America, 2012, it really isn't. To prove that assertion, I challenge you to think of one area of your life that is not regulated or controlled by some form of civil government.

It is involved when your baby is born, in filling out the Birth Certificate; and, *heavily* involved in the healthcare industry that'll oversee the delivery. Even if you choose to birth at home, or with a midwife, stand by for government hurdles at least, if not blatant interference and/or intimidation.

When you die, your loved ones will pay inheritance taxes and the mortician will have to follow all manner of civil regulations in the disposal of your remains. So, literally, from womb to tomb the government's fingers are in your business.

I'm the first to say, yes, it'd be great to not have to get tangled up with the government and its always-attendant politics. ***But they will not allow this.***

You may not want to get involved, but their tentacles are already wrapped around everything you do. From the light-bulbs and toilets you can install in your own home, to the food you purchase, to the water or milk or whatever you may drink, to the very air you breathe, the American government is regulating all of it.

What this Objection is really saying, therefore, is, "Let's all do our best to ignore the tyranny we live with, and see if, by so doing, they'll basically leave us alone, so that we can busy ourselves with churchy things (which are also regulated, by the way.)"

There is already evidence, though, that it may be too late for this sort of thing. There are videos, easily available on the internet right now, that visually document instances in which Christians who take to public street corners to preach the Gospel are then confronted by police and either told to shut it down, or are arrested outright.

What shall we say about this sort of thing, which by all accounts is happening in America with increasing frequency? How will the current Objection deal with this dilemma?

We've reached the point where it's no longer unheard of, or even all that unusual, for the "politics" to stomp on the scene with its iron feet and silence the Gospel. *Now what?*

Fall back some more, maybe? Give more ground? Hey, they haven't found a way to regulate your prayer-life yet: Maybe we could modify the Objection to, "Don't get tangled up in politics; just pray where they can't find you."

In a country in which politicians of both parties have reached into *everything*, it is worse than naïve to urge Christians to "not get involved."

But the final reason why this Objection utterly fails is that it betrays an appalling lack of understanding about the nature and reach of the Gospel of Jesus Christ, when it is faithfully preached in the power of the Holy Spirit. ***Read the book of Acts.*** Time and again, the preachers of the Gospel found themselves tangled up with politics. The reason was, because the true Gospel doesn't stay in church: it changes *everything*, including whole cultures, along with their governments.

Those first preachers of the Gospel in Acts didn't get in trouble so much for creating a "new religion." What they got in trouble for was announcing the dominion of "another king, Jesus." (Acts 17:7)

What this Objection fails to realize is that the assertion that "Jesus is Lord" is not politically neutral. Rulers in rebellion toward God hear it as a threat. It is right for them to hear it as a threat because it is. More than a threat, it is their downfall, their doom, and even if they don't admit it, despots everywhere since the time of Christ have instinctively known it to be so.

As we have seen above, the civil magistrate was ordained as God's minister, His deacon. That right there ought to be enough to let us know that it's foolish to separate God from politics. It's all His.

Every tyrant will answer to Him. This is a big part of why we should pray for kings and rulers and all who are in authority. They will stand before God and give an account. They therefore are in desperate need of the Gospel.

Was David getting tangled up in politics when he urged Gentile kings to "Kiss the Son," and to escape God's wrath by trusting in Him? (Psalms 2:12) Was John the Baptist not focusing on the Gospel when he rebuked the pagan Edomite, King Herod, with the Law of God for marrying his brother's wife? (Mark 6:17-19)

As with trying to separate from all sinners everywhere, you'll have to actually leave the planet to make this Objection a workable reality.

Objection: "So, are you saying we should all become criminals and anarchists as we disobey the government?"

No. That's not what I'm saying.

I haven't suggested that. I am suggesting that if we recognize that we live in a God-hating tyranny, we need to set ourselves in opposition to that tyranny. We refuse to recognize the legitimacy of it.

That doesn't mean we become law-breakers and villains.

We must be careful not to point out the tiny sliver in Caesar's eye while ignoring the plank hanging out of our own. I mean that the way we determine whether our government has become tyrannical is by assessing their attitude and obedience toward God's commandments. At the same time, this very standard applies to us as well.

You really forfeit your right to complain about the government's law-breaking when you yourself are living in a manner that defies God's commands.

If we recognize that our rulers have become tyrannical antichrist figures, and therefore illegitimate to govern under God, this doesn't leave the Christian citizen with no law to follow. We are still responsible to God. We still obey Him.

I am not suggesting or advocating anarchy. I am saying that all of us, including the shadowy denizens of Washington, D.C., ought to keep God's commandments.

Objection: Joseph, Daniel, and Esther all lived under pagan rulers and God was able to exalt them and make them thrive in that condition. Scripture does not show them doing things to resist or oppose the kings of their day. Therefore, Christians need not oppose wicked rulers in our day.

On first blush, this may seem like a formidable argument. But as we consider the details of each of these stories, I think we'll see that they actually *argue in favor of the thesis of this book.*

In Joseph's case, he went from slave, to prisoner, to ruler over all of Egypt with lightning-fast speed. Scripture's testimony about his position, once God had caused him to prosper, is that the only way in which Pharaoh was greater than Joseph was in the fact that Pharaoh was the one who sat on the throne (Genesis 41:40.) Joseph, therefore, was in charge of everything. To declare that Joseph didn't oppose the pagan government of his day is to miss the fact that, for all intents, he *was* the government of his day! It's a bit like trying to point out that Tom Landry never won a game against the Dallas Cowboys throughout his entire head-coaching career.

With Daniel, the first time we see him, he and his friends are putting themselves at some risk for undermining the king's orders concerning their diets, for the sake of their own consciences (Daniel 1.) Later, of course, he defies the foolish pagan ruler outright and gets himself thrown into the lion's den (Daniel 6.) He also boldly prophesied that one king would go crazy and be temporarily deposed (Daniel 4) and similarly announced that the end of another had come (Daniel 5.) He did this to their faces.

These are not the actions of a milquetoast meekly acquiescing to power. It wouldn't be shocking to find that the kings in question thought that all these things were rather seditious.

We also need to remember, in Daniel's case, that he was well-versed in the prophecies that preceded him, and he knew how long Judah's captivity was supposed to last (Daniel 9:2.) He therefore had a specific word from the Lord that told him when the yoke of the pagans would be broken. That is not the case in modern America.

In addition, we note that after courageously prophesying hard things to two separate kings, Daniel was made the chief official over 120 princes who ruled all of Persia. The pagans reported to him (Daniel 6:1-2) and they hated it (Daniel 6:4.) So when one objects that Daniel didn't oppose the wicked government of his day, first of all, his actions say otherwise, and secondly, he took the whole thing *over!*

Is that the proposed definition of "submission to authority?" If so, I'm in favor of it.

Esther, in similar fashion as Joseph, went from being a young member of a slave-race to someplace right up near the top rung of Persia's power ladder, practically overnight. Even so, we've missed the whole plot of her story if we fail to see, at its culmination, that she took courage and refused to simply *submit* to the king's atrocious command concerning her people.

In fact, she developed and implemented a plan to *oppose* that wickedness, using all the tools available to her at the time. Let's not forget that as a direct result of this opposition of hers, the idolatrous Persians suffered a hefty military defeat at the hands of the Jews, and the tyrannical government official, Haman, was hanged.

All three of these stories, therefore, rather than encourage Christians to simply bow down, or bend over, for cruel tyrants, actually teach the opposite. They teach that by depending on God's power and grace, not only can God's people prosper in wicked systems, but they can even expect God to exalt them *over those systems* as they remain faithful to Him alone.

PART THREE: APPLICATION AND CONCLUSION

Well, you've made it this far. You almost certainly fall into one of the following categories.

Category A: You are convinced my cheese has slipped off the cracker. You disagree with everything, and have from the beginning. You continued reading because you couldn't look away, like passing a car accident on the road. In this case, thanks so much for your time. I'm truly sorry if you think it was a waste.

Category B: You are about halfway on board with me. In fact, you'd be hard-pressed to say what it is that keeps you from being fully on board, but something does. Please keep reading. I suspect that part of what is bugging you is that you know, maybe instinctively, that if I'm right about all this, that's going to demand something from you. And that something may not be comfortable.

Category C: You think I've got it basically right. Now that we agree, it begs the question: So what do we do about it? We know it is right to oppose tyrants, but what would that look like for us in America right now? That's what we need to talk about.

Category D: You think I'm brilliant, a wonderful writer and teacher, God's gift to the modern church. In which case, Mom, I told you it was okay if you didn't want to read this!

WHERE DO WE GO FROM HERE?

I was recently speaking with a combat veteran from the Afghan war. He is an expert marksman in the US Army and, in fact, trains his fellow soldiers in the use of firearms.

Out of curiosity, on the spur of the moment, I asked him this question, "What would your first, best piece of advice be for someone who really wants to be able to use a gun to defend his home?"

He deliberated for all of about half a second.

He said, matter-of-factly, "It's all about attitude. It really is."

Attitude.

My friend stressed that approaching a firefight is really more about mindset than it is about the other "usual suspects" like strategy, time spent on the range, equipment choice, or technical things like making sure you breathe correctly as you squeeze (don't pull) the trigger. Not that those things are un-important, but that *attitude* is far and away at the top of the stack.

His best advice for home defense with a gun, therefore, was to make sure all of your mental reservations are settled way, *way* before the shooting starts. If you're walking through your home at night with your pistol, because you think maybe you heard someone break a window or something, and internally you are dealing with serious, lingering qualms about the prospect of shooting and killing an intruder…you are practically beaten right at the beginning. You are not defending anything: you are begging to be the second shooter, not the first. And the one who goes second is normally known as the first victim.

So settle it now, while you're thinking soberly and the sun is shining.

I say all that to suggest that this issue of attitude is crucial to learning how to resist tyrants. Settle it now. If you have qualms, deal with them as a Christian, through prayer, Bible study, and trusted, godly counsel.

Resistance to tyrants is obedience to God. Either you believe that or not; and, you either believe it applies in the current situation or it doesn't. But get it figured out, while you're not being harassed, and the sun is shining.

When you do, you may well experience what is known in modern parlance as a paradigm-shift. That happens when the acceptance of a truth in one area of your life manages to unexpectedly change the way *everything* looks to you, in every area. It can feel like waking up in the morning and suddenly realizing that the sky is blue. You knew it before, of course, but it's so darn *blue* today!

You need to get there first, before discussions like this one can really move forward.

Once you do, though, Christian citizen, it shouldn't shock you to hear that your resistance to tyrants should be a recognizably *Christian* resistance to tyrants. And that means your struggle against evil in *government* is to be handled in basically the same way that Christians struggle against evil in other forms.

Just because a tactic works, doesn't mean we get to use it. The unbelievers have made an art form, for example, out of digging up dirt on their political enemies and using it to smear them. This is very often effective. It's also a sleazy, dishonorable way of doing business. Christians should set the bar a tad higher for themselves than that.

Sure, maybe it's a little heartbreaking to come to the realization that you can no longer be the sort of patriot your country celebrated this last July 4th, 2012. It can't be "My country, right or wrong," anymore. That was never anything other than false patriotism anyway. That was nationalism, not patriotism, and it is idolatrous.

Not July 4th, 2012, but rather, July 4th, 1776. There is a difference in the Americanism that is featured in the chest-beating, red-white-and-blue ballads of modern Country music, and the genuine American patriotism of the *Declaration of Independence*. Your patriotism must be the latter.

Resist as a *CHRISTIAN*

A famous preacher from a couple centuries ago, Robert Murray McCheyne, once said, "The greatest gift I can give my congregation is my godliness." I think he was talking about the importance of genuinely living the life he was urging his listeners to live. We've all had our fill of "men of God" who are fantastic when it comes to talking the talk. Then we find out the famous pastor is leading a secret life that involves his wearing of women's underwear.

I hope for you, Christian patriot, that you are blessed to be in a church led by men of God who quietly and firmly lead lives that are consistent with their message. To be part of a church like that is a wonderful gift.

I mention this to illustrate a principle. What is good to find inside a church is also needed (and severely lacking) among those who claim to be patriotic Americans. A Christian pastor who is secretly enslaved to sin is axiomatically not taking a principled stand for righteousness, no matter what he says from the pulpit. In the same way, a Christian patriot who is unconcerned with obeying God in his personal life, is really incapable of resisting tyranny. If you are a slave within your own soul, your outward, political fight for liberty is paper-thin hypocrisy.

[This is the terminal illness, by the way, that runs throughout much of the modern libertarian movement. It is largely populated by atheists, and atheism can provide no objective reason for believing that liberty is better than tyranny. It's a matter of mere personal preference. However, it also runs rampant within underground patriot movements, militias, and the Tea Party movement, this outward call for government to back off while inwardly, voluntarily serving the sickest despot of them all, the lust to sin. These tend to give lip-service to faith, by appending the adjective of Christian onto whatever it is they've decided to do.

In contrast with all of this, the apostle James referred to the Law of God as "the perfect Law of Liberty." (Jas 1:25) Even as we acknowledge (joyfully!) that we cannot be saved by keeping the Law, and law-keeping is not what "keeps" us saved once we've been converted; still, it is clear that Christian freedom in this life is a freedom *under* God's commandments, not freedom *from* them.

Not only is this the basis of personal liberty, but the only sound basis for cultural liberty, or freedom as a nation. I think our founding fathers recognized this.

To explore these concepts more fully, I recommend you get a copy of the book *Law ana Liberty* by R.J. Rushdoony.]

There is only one avenue to freedom from this inward, secret slavery to the devil's tyranny. That one avenue is Jesus Christ, who claimed to be the way, the truth and the life. When He submitted Himself to death upon the cross, it was as your substitute. Crucifixion was capital punishment, Roman style. It was the sentence reserved for the worst criminals.

The Bible says that you and I fully deserve that sentence of death, because we have spent our lives breaking the laws of God, the great King, and acting as hostile rebels within His kingdom. Every sin we've ever committed is an act of insurrection, an attempt to cast the Creator of the universe down from His throne. If He were to pronounce us "guilty" and exact the fitting punishment upon us, death and Hell would be only right.

But the Bible tells us that this God, this great King, who has a right to rule and to punish rebels, is also good and kind and full of mercy. He sent His only Son, the Lord Jesus, to take your place. He willingly suffered the punishment for crimes against God that you and I committed.

The blood that He shed, dying in your place, is the eternal price of your freedom. He had every right to destroy you, but He died to save you instead.

God then raised Him from the dead on the third day, and Scripture says Jesus has been seated at His right hand, the place of ultimate authority, and He is now the one who rules everything as King of kings, and Lord of lords.

One day, He will return and put an end to all things, judging every individual who has ever been born for the things done in the flesh. Now is the time to escape the judgment that you have earned, that you deserve. Now is the time to flee from the wrath to come.

Friend, if you are reading this and you know, just between you and God, that you have never received this complete forgiveness, let me beg you to put this book down right now and simply call out to the living Lord Jesus Christ to save you. Tell Him you want to be free from sin's slavery, and to serve Him with joy, and without fear, forever. It is His own unshakeable promise that "whosoever shall call upon the name of the Lord shall be saved." (Romans 10:13)

Only when these things have honestly been resolved will you be ready to resist the modern tyranny we live under as a Christian.

RESIST as a Christian

Christian patriot, now that our minds are right, our wills fully resolved, and our hearts washed clean through Christ, now we're ready to join the resistance and really take steps toward the dethroning of the tyranny we find over us. As I mentioned above, for a Christian to oppose evil in government is a thing that is not unlike opposing evil as he finds it in his family, or church, or workplace, etc.

Thing is, that opposition looks foolish to the world, and seems impotent to the bloodthirsty. Our weapons are not carnal, and so carnal people will react to them (at least initially) with scorn and laughter.

The laughter tends to stop, though, once they start to experience the truth that these same weapons are mighty in God for the pulling down of strongholds.

Despots and tyrants have historically persecuted Christians, not on a lark, not for a good time on the weekend, but because they felt themselves threatened. Ask the persecutors and they'll uniformly say they *have to do it*, purely as a defensive measure: because everything they care about is threatened by these Christ-followers. Nothing will be stable until they are wiped out, etc.

It's time to be that sort of Christian, friends. It is reported that Sam Houston, the giant of Texas history, once said he preferred to know that 10,000 Mexican troops had crossed into Texas, than to hear that ten circuit-riding Methodist preachers had done so. It's been a looong, long time since any American politician was at all afraid of what havoc might be wreaked in his territory by a Gospel preacher. Too long. We need to strive be that kind of Christian, the kind that strikes fear into tyrants by doing nothing more than being consistent witnesses.

How do we get there from here? The whole Bible is about answering that kind of question. But that's a big book. For now, here are some summary-type suggestions. It'll be up to you and your local body of believers and leaders to formulate details where they're needed.

1. How do we get there? First, repent of not having gotten there already. It's no one's fault but our own that we haven't yet arrived there.

2. It's not enough to be readers of the Bible. It's not enough, even, to be students. You must become a devotee. Knowing Scripture must become your passion, just as it behooved a medieval knight to become passionate about practicing with a sword and shield.

3. Pray without ceasing. Make prayer your weapon against tyranny. God is the one who casts down one king and exalts another. *Start begging Him to do that!* Make the Psalms your prayer book. Learn to pray through those inspired prayers and hymns: Including the so-called Imprecatory Psalms, those in which the author is calling on God to rebuke, curse, and even destroy his enemies.

4. Get educated. If I could recommend a couple of books to you, let me suggest Greg L. Bahnsen's *By This Standard*, as well as Rushdoony's *The Institutes of Biblical Law*.

It makes no sense to criticize tyrants for their idiotic and evil policies, if you have no Bible-based suggestions to advocate in their place. These books will help greatly. Use this knowledge to educate others, especially your children.

5. Make yourself a nuisance by criticizing tyrants for their idiotic and evil policies. Whatever audience God gives you, by whatever means, give the enemy no rest. Let him have it, loudly as possible, though seasoned with grace. My personal goal is to live in such a way that when God does finally call me home, the armies of hell will breathe a sigh of relief and say, "Man! I'm glad *that's* over!"

6. Join with other Christian patriots who feel the same way and are serious about these things. Lots of you attend dumb churches, frankly, filled with sheeple, and fattened shepherds (or worse, hipsters) who avoid controversy like the plague. Stop that. Better to fellowship with a small handful that is legitimately faithful than dance to Hell as part of a large, harlot congregation.

7. Whatever it is that God has given you to do, do it with all your might. For two reasons. One, this glorifies God. Two, the devil hates it. Pursuing the God-given calling on your life, whether as a missionary in foreign lands, or as a homeschooling mom right here, is an act of defiance.

8. If we must resist, and be in opposition continually, and I think we must, let's do it in a way that makes the other side wonder what we've got to be so happy about. Strive, yes. Fight, yes. But, as Douglas Wilson has suggested, fight like a Musketeer from the movies, who swings his sword with a hearty, "Ha, ha!" and manages to make fun of his enemies while he does. Humor needs to sit right beside Truth in your quiver of arrows. One of the first things the enemy would take from you is the Joy of the Lord. This is ground you must hold, no matter what.

9. Be a gospel-centered believer. It is, according to Paul, the radical message of salvation by grace through faith that is, "the power of God unto salvation." (Romans 1:16) This power needs to be blasted at the gates of hell in a constant barrage.

But, you ask, is there any other kind of believer than what you label a "gospel-centered" one?

Um, sadly, yes there is. And the reason you don't know what I mean is because being other-than-gospel-centered has become so prevalent in our day, it is the new normal.

10. Civil disobedience is a legitimate expression of Christian resistance. The key is, though, if you're going to be involved in this sort of action, you need to be willing to accept the consequences, whatever they are. Those consequences are rarely comfortable, so keep this in mind.

11. On the question of armed resistance, let me simply say, in imitation of our founders before us: It ought to be our last option. That is, like the signers of the *Declaration*, we need to be able to say that all other means have been honestly tried and have manifestly failed. It needs to be the option we hate thinking about, and the one we would only consider, literally, at the *last*, as a regrettable measure of self-defense. It is a Biblical principle that if you are attacked, you are allowed to respond.

But, that said, this "last option" really does need to be an *option*. By calling it the last of such options, everyone should understand that we are not thereby taking it off the table. It's the *last* option, but it's a *live* one.

On this note as well, I think wisdom demands that we not "go there" unless there is some reasonable, legitimate shot at victory. There's nothing necessarily righteous about going down in a blaze of glory, or committing suicide via a hail of bullets.

There may in fact come a time for mass, armed resistance. If it does, we'll need to do our best to be something other than complete morons about it. Winning is a much better goal than to simply die with your boots on.

Speaking of recipes for becoming the sort of Christian that the tyrants will eventually see as a significant threat, my faulty, feeble list above happily yields and gives place to a similar list of to-do items that the Apostle Paul (who knew a thing or two about standing firm in the face of evil) wrote in Romans 12:9-21. Major in *these* things, and the combined forces of hell will tremble at your approach, I guarantee it:

> *Let love be genuine.*
> *Abhor what is evil; hold fast to what is good.*
> *Love one another with brotherly affection.*
> *Outdo one another in showing honor.*
> *Do not be slothful in zeal, be fervent in spirit, serve the Lord.*
> *Rejoice in hope, be patient in tribulation, be constant in prayer.*
> *Contribute to the needs of the saints and seek to show hospitality.*
> *Bless those who persecute you; bless and do not curse them.*
> *Rejoice with those who rejoice, weep with those who weep.*
> *Live in harmony with one another.*
> *Do not be haughty, but associate with the lowly.*

Never be wise in your own sight.

Repay no one evil for evil, but give thought to do what is honorable in the sight of all.

If possible, so far as it depends on you, live peaceably with all.

Beloved, never avenge yourselves, but leave it to the wrath of God, for it is written, "Vengeance is mine, I will repay, says the Lord."

To the contrary, "if your enemy is hungry, feed him; if he is thirsty, give him something to drink; for by so doing you will heap burning coals on his head."

Do not be overcome by evil, but overcome evil with good.

May our good and gracious God see fit in our day to raise up a mighty army of saints who take passages like this one above as a battle-plan, and then go do it.

Amen.

THE AUTHOR

Gordan Runyan is the pastor of Immanuel Baptist Church in Tucumcari, New Mexico. He lives with his high school sweetheart, a gullible young lady he tricked into marrying him in 1985. They have three beautiful daughters and something just shy of a thousand cats, along with one nervous bird.

He is a veteran, having served during the first Persian Gulf War (Operation Desert Storm) as part of the US Navy's nuclear submarine fleet. His name appears online as a friend of the Founders Ministry and 9Marks, and also on Pastor Chuck Baldwin's list of Black Regiment pastors.

He is the author of the Christian military thriller, *Prowl*; a seven week daily devotional gleaned from Psalms 119 called *As In All Riches*; a mini-book on the Doctrines of Grace called *Clarified Calvinism: What It Is, What It Isn't*; and an article titled, *Seven Reasons Why Christian Patriots Should Give Libertarianism a 2nd Look*. These are all available at Amazon.com if you'll enter his name into the search engine there. He is also an occasional writer for the popular news/opinion blog, The Freedom Outpost (freedomoutpost.com.)

You may email comments and death-threats to Gordan at **reformnm@yahoo.com**. You can also find him on Facebook.

HAPPY SEIGE

This little book is a volley aimed at the walls of the godless establishment, brought to you with great joy by a shadowy, secret organization called Happy Siege.

We are a terribly mysterious group which believes that Christian pastors ought to be decent communicators, and Christians who can communicate ought to darn well do so by churning out books.

We seek to see all of life renewed, reformed, reconstructed (as it were) by the principles of the Word of God, to the glory of our Captain, the Lord Jesus Christ. This is our rebellious, dastardly intention, and if it were possible to track us down, you might find us discussing it with enthusiasm and laughter, possibly in a smoke-filled room wherein dusky spirits congregate in tinkling glasses.

If none of this has caused you to run screaming into the night, and you are a Christian who can string some pithy phrases together (and, no I wasn't lisping there) but you feel like you could use some help getting ready to publish, find us. All the clues you might need to do that have already appeared somewhere in this book.

Cheers!

Happy Siege:
"Have fun storming the castle!"

Made in the USA
Lexington, KY
27 May 2016